Joro Spiders

don't scare me

Written by CHRISTEN JESCHKE

Freiling PUBLISHING

Published by Freiling Publishing, a division of Freiling Agency, LLC.

P.O. Box 1264, Warrenton, VA 20188

www.FreilingPublishing.com

ISBN 978-1-956267-52-5

Printed in the United States of America
Designed by Debbie Lewis

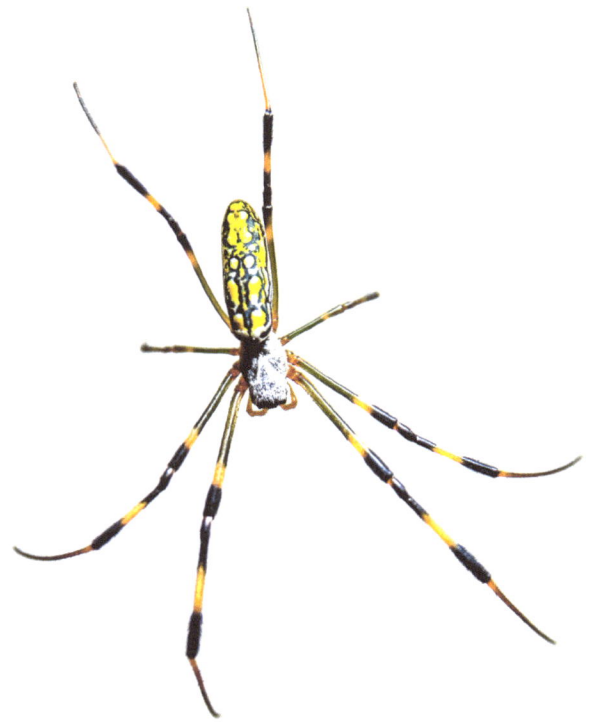

In loving remembrance of my
"Grandmommie" Betty Little Morey
who gave me my first
and funniest spider memory.

Joro spiders are awesome,
so intricate, and nice.

Here are some Joro facts
to make you think twice.

Joro spiders are arachnids, complete with eight legs.

This air-breathing arthropod spins silk sacs for eggs.

The egg sac is strong, made in a circular shape.

It's as big as a golf ball or small as a grape.

The hatchlings come forth in the warmth of the spring.

What will the next phase of their life-cycle bring?

Tiny spiderlings
climb, stretching
legs to the sky,

Casting gossamer
parachutes that float
and that fly.

A technique called
ballooning creates a
silk glider,

Making travel a breeze
for this high-flying
spider.

Joros soar on air currents,
then stop where they land.

Eventually growing as big as your hand.

The male spider is smaller–its markings quite plain.

The female is a beauty–her colors entertain.

DID YOU KNOW: Joro spiders produce giant three-dimensional webs that can be up to ten feet deep.

With striping
that's black, bright
yellow, or blue,

Her abdomen's
splashed in a red
vibrant hue.

DID YOU KNOW: Female Joro spiders display a signature blush red marking on the underside of their abdomen.

Watching them weave is
such marvelous fun.

Their webs shine like gold
in the rays of the sun.

DID YOU KNOW: Joro spiders eat mosquitoes,
stink bugs, flies, and other small insects or prey
that become entangled in their webs.

Basket-shaped orbs spun
between two different trees.

Webs lure in winged prey
on the breath of the breeze.

Joros eat stink bugs and other pests too.

Turning bothersome insects into liquified goo.

These spiders are big, but there's no need for fright.

Their fangs are too tiny to pierce with a bite.

DID YOU KNOW: Joro spiders are passive, timid spiders who usually run and hide when their webs are disturbed.

Joro spiders don't scare me.
They are gentle and kind.

Observe them with care–
this magnificent find.

www.ingramcontent.com/pod-product-compliance
Lightning Source LLC
LaVergne TN
LVHW072133070426
835513LV00002B/96